Arran

sixty best views

Arran
sixty best views

First Published April 2018
by
Allan Wright Photographic

www.allanwrightphoto.com

ISBN 978-1-905683-95-6

Printed by Skleniarz, Poland

ALLANWRIGHT
PHOTOGRAPHIC

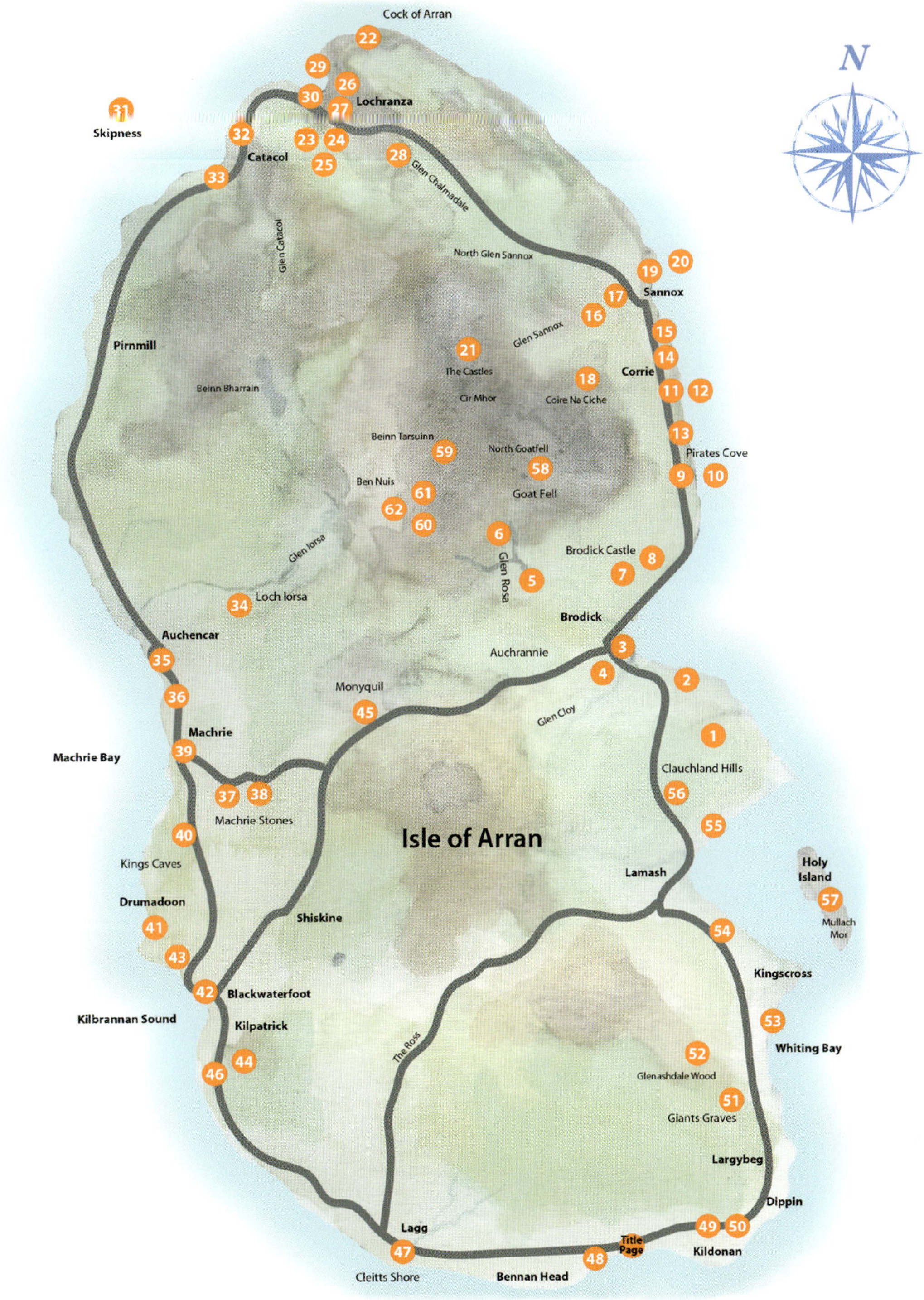

N
Cock of Arran
22
29
26
30
27
Lochranza
31
Skipness
32
23
24
Catacol
25
28
Glen Chalmadale
33
Glen Catacol
North Glen Sannox
19
20
Sannox
17
16
15
Pirnmill
21
Glen Sannox
14
The Castles
18
Corrie
11
12
Beinn Bharrain
Cir Mhor
Coire Na Ciche
13
Beinn Tarsuinn
59
North Goatfell
Pirates Cove
58
9
10
Ben Nuis
61
Goat Fell
62
60
6
Glen Iorsa
Brodick Castle
8
Glen Rosa
7
5
34
Loch Iorsa
Brodick
Auchencar
3
35
Auchrannie
4
2
Monyquil
36
45
Glen Cloy
1
Machrie
39
Machrie Bay
Clauchland Hills
37
38
56
Machrie Stones
55
40
Isle of Arran
Kings Caves
Holy Island
Lamash
Drumadoon
57
Shiskine
54
Mullach Mor
41
43
Kingscross
42
Blackwaterfoot
Kilbrannan Sound
Kilpatrick
53
Whiting Bay
The Ross
52
44
46
Glenashdale Wood
51
Giants Graves
Largybeg
Dippin
49
50
Lagg
Title Page
47
48
Kildonan
Cleitts Shore
Bennan Head

Preface

The world is made up of two types of people; those who have been to Arran and those who have not, this book is for them both. In my travels I often have conversations about what Arran means to people, often it seems either they remain charmed from childhood experiences, or they feel a bit embarrassed because they have not managed to get there yet.

The "Scotland in miniature" cliché it possesses was dreamed up by the image merchants in the world of marketing some time ago. This identity has become embedded in the national consciousness and so living up to such a tag line is a tall order when you consider the vast range of attributes the rest of Scotland presents to the traveller. Either an objective review or a misty eyed embrace will confirm that this catch line is in fact truly deserved.

A short sail across the Clyde estuary from the Ayrshire port of Ardrossan is actually transportation of two kinds. Apart from the obvious kind, the traveller is also transported by an unseen and bewitching process that delivers you into something called "island time". This is when things slow down, cares diminish and nature captivates. A hungrily persistent anxiety might emerge along the lines of "where do I go next?", otherwise Arran is a serious chill out zone and it is right there, just 2-3 hours from Scotland's main population centres.

This modest portfolio edition represents edited highlights from over 20 years of photographic exploration. The work is by nature, personal and subjective and cannot claim to be comprehensive. Every location featured possesses a special sense of place. I regard it as my task to tune in to and deliver this sense. To process of creating a deserving image is to enter into a game of chance, but the chance factor is underpinned by calculations aimed at shortening the odds of achieving a desirable result. Utilising the rich spectrum of Scottish West Coast light as it plays out its merry dance across the land through all the seasons, the possibilities are unlimited. When elements conspire to bring a landscape to life like this, I acknowledge a quiet sense of privilege.

To talk photo-speak for a moment; finding a good angle is a large part of the art of landscape photography but without the magic ingredient, light, things will not transcend to create anything special. An awareness of the path of the sun during all four seasons and the quality of light it produces during the rhythm of the day is second nature to the landscape photographer. In this sense I could revisit all these featured locations again and be presented with a distinctively different set of qualities.

Preface

To talk photo-speak for a moment; finding a good angle is a large part of the art of landscape photography but without the magic ingredient, light, things will not transcend to create anything special. An awareness of the path of the sun during all four seasons and the quality of light it produces during the rhythm of the day is second nature to the landscape photographer. In this sense I could revisit all these featured locations again and be presented with a distinctively different set of qualities.

Arran offers wilderness in abundance; a shoreline of great beauty & diversity perfect for a meditative ramble, that with dramatic glens with tumbling burns to uplift the spirit. Trek through wooded foothills into the heart of its ancient mountains and you will find tranquil lochans guarded by towering, rugged peaks. If a dose of solitude is an essential to nourish both heart and soul, Arran will also provide. Delve into history and pre-history with castles, forts and Neolithic stones then simply take some contemplative time travel to further lose yourself. The atmosphere in the towns and villages is welcoming with world class facilities and the best of Scottish hospitality to complete the inventory of reasons to spend as much time as possible losing yourself on this wonderful island.

The images in this book are sequenced very roughly as an anti-clockwise circumnavigation of the island starting at Brodick, with an ascent into the mountains at the end. I have attempted to define the locations of each photograph by means of a corresponding page number on the map which appears on the previous page to this. I would be delighted to think that this book might function as a sort of "ad hoc" guide book. If an image transmits a special sense of place that the viewer feels a connection with then, with a little sleuthing, he or she could navigate to the same location and have an equally joyful experience as I had.

In my experience Arran offers a very intense and varied package of life-affirming opportunities within its 167 square miles all of them contributing to supporting its seemingly grandiose claim on the title "Scotland in miniature".

Allan Wright

April 2018

Goat Fell and the Tarsuinn Ridge tower over Brodick Bay while the MV Caledonian Isles departs for Ardrossan.

The sleek lines of the MV Caledonian Isles partner perfectly with the classic profile of Goat Fell.

Rosa Water meanders from the heart of the island through the wooded slopes of Glen Rosa. In confluence with the Cloy Water, it enters the sea at Brodick Beach.

From the Auchrannie Resort.
With a nod to the exotic, a tropical silhouette sets off the familiar profile of Torr nan Dearc at the head of Glen Cloy.

Rugged peaks such as Ben Nuis beckon walkers along the easy ramble to the heart of Glen Rosa.

For many, Glen Rosa is characterised by the iconic 'Rockpool'
Effortlessly photogenic,the glacial boulder and plunging crystal waters are perfectly offset by the jagged peak of mighty Cir Mhor in the distance.

Built in 1510, Brodick Castle is central to the island's heritage. Formerly seat of Dukes of Hamilton, it is now in the care of the National Trust for Scotland. Its impressive sandstone-construction structure is wonderfully complemented by the surrounding woodland garden.

The granite boulders strewn along the red sandstone shore south of the village of Corrie are a compelling sight. The textures and abstract designs are nature's work of genius.

The Arran ferry and the profile of Mullach Beag on Holy Isle team up with a clutch of granite boulders on Corrie shore.

With its two mini harbours and all the idyllic promise a coastal fishing village could offer, Corrie Village has an immediate charm. Sheltered from the Atlantic and nestling beneath the core mountain range, in scenic value it has few equals.

Atmospheric first light catches the detail of a reproduction Viking longship moored within South Corrie Harbour.

Deep and glossy reflections in North Corrie Harbour.
Nestling beneath Goat Fell is a village sweetened with fresh summer colours.

Pirate's Cove, Corrie Shore. A small inshore vessel works the creels whilst a big sky rises out of the Ayrshire coast.

Glen Sannox. A lyrical swirling of morning mist evokes special appreciation in this, the fairest of glens.
A long but easy amble penetrates this magical place to the core of the Arran Mountains.

Even in stark winter plumage, Glen Sannox can leave you spellbound.

Viewed here from Coire Na Ciche, aka The Devil's Punchbowl, the Allt a Chapuill burn flows beneath the peak Cioch Na H-Oighe, aka The Bastion.

First light caresses the rocks on the shore from Sannox Point.
From left: The Bastion, Witch's Step, Caisteal Abhail (The Castles) and Cir Mhor.

Trekking an ascent of the North Glen Sannox Burn ultimately delivers the finest of vistas from among the rugged ridge structures known as The Castles (Caisteal Abhail).
The dominating pinnacle of Cir Mhor steals the show.

The shoreline between Newton Point at Lochranza and the North Sannox Estuary picnic area is a challenging ramble. Near the northerly point of the 'Cock of Arran' is an impressive geological cliff feature called 'Fallen Rocks'.

Descending by road from the heights of Glen Chalmadale, Lochranza feels like it is in a world of its own. With its fjord–like topography, its tranquil bay offers multiple facets to be discovered.

Lochranza Castle predominates as a focal point.
Viewed here from Coille Mor, the perspective reveals Newton Point and emphasises its close relationship with the Kintyre Peninsula.

Big summer skies rise behind the castle, and the shore of Lochranza is festooned with thrift.

The sunset stag party on The Haven shore of Lochranza is a fairly routine event.

The malt whisky distillery of Lochranza was founded in 1994. Revered by connoisseurs, its golden dram has since become a global brand.

There is a wonderful co-existence between humanity and the red deer herd that roam freely within the natural habitats in and around Lochranza Bay.

Lochranza is an ideal venue for seeing the day out with its long tidal reach, plentiful shore detail and reliable sunsets.

From the high ground above Skipness on the Kintyre mainland, the island can be seen in its singular entirety.

Colloquially known as 'The Twelve Apostles', this row of traditional fishermen's cottages defines the unique character of Catacol village.

The luminescent aquamarine of high summer fringes the shore of the idyllic Catacol Village in the far north-west of the island.

Possessing qualities of a small Highland glen, the environs of Loch Iorsa make for a tranquil ramble.

Seen here guarded by thistles, the island's tallest Neolithic monolith at Auchencar is known as 'The Druid Stone'.

Last light bursts through heavy storm clouds, momentarily dramatising the broad expanse of Machrie Bay.

The prehistoric site at Machrie Moor is richly endowed with Neolithic stones and stone circles.
The sublime setting and the awesome scale of these four sandstone monoliths can leave you transfixed with a deep sense of the ancient.

Granite textures on the Machrie shore set off a wispy high summer sky.

From the gentle trek to The Kings' Caves, the twin summits of Beinn Lochain and Chaorach sport a headband of mist to complement the classic vista of Machrie Bay.

Viewed from the twelve-hole Shiskine golf course is the site of the island's largest iron-age fort at Drumadoon Point, Blackwaterfoot. Shortly before sundown, the columnar geology glows amber in the low sun..

The cutest of harbours here at Blackwaterfoot responds well to a September sunset behind Kintyre Peninsula.

Looking out to the Kilbrannan Sound from Blackwaterfoot Beach at dusk. A lone drifter in silhouette seems to float on a golden haze.

Radiant in winter plumage, the dominating peak of Beinn Nuis rises behind the hamlet of Kilpatrick Point just south of Shiskine.

At the start of 'The String' road, Monyquil Farm nestles in the lee of the high ground leading to the high peaks of Creag Nam Mear and Beinn Nuis.

From the rugged coastal trail at Kilpatrick Point, crisp winter light highlights the broad settlement of Blackwaterfoot.

A journey round the southern coast of the island is enhanced by persistent and captivating glimpses of iconic Ailsa Craig.
In the foregound, a contented cormorant colony catches the last rays on the Cleats Shore by Lagg / Kilmory.

Few shoreline strolls can deliver compositions that offer such a powerful fusion of wildlife and seascape as the beach walk from Kildonan to Bennan Head.

The definitive conical form of Ailsa Craig punctuates the horizon as an Ayrshire dawn breaks across the Clyde Estuary.
The tiny islet of Pladda, with its working lighthouse, simply owns the inshore waters of Kildonan.

Kildonan. Woodland and rough pasture in the foreground support the distant Bennan Head cliffs as they awaken to the golden rays of a winter sunrise.

The view from the archaeological site known as the 'Giant's Graves' offers a perfect perspective to define Whiting Bay's topographical relationship to Holy Isle.

As part of a circular trail to the Giant's Graves from Whiting Bay, a visit to the magnificent Glenashdale Falls offers intimate contact with one of the jewels of the island's natural heritage.

The shore at Whiting Bay witnesses nature's blessing upon the Buddhist retreat on Holy Isle.

With its tidy ribbon settlement and the ever-present Goat Fell peak, the view from the road as one descends into Lamlash is an everyday classic.

Even from within the environs of Lamlash, Holy Isle as a subject has an infinite selection of moods, angles and compositions to explore.

Golf is big on Arran, and the course at Lamlash has scenic quality in abundance.

From the summit of Mullach Mor, the highest point on Holy Isle.
In summer splendour it offers a fine perspective across toClauchlands Point and the Arran mountains beyond.

The Goat Fell climb is the biggest draw for walkers. Here on the northern ridge, last light enhances the rugged beauty of this stunning mountain habitat.

Viewed from Coire a' Bhradain high above Glen Rosa, an enticing jagged ridge skylines the connection between the twin peaks of Beinn Tarsuinn and Beinn Nuis.

Exceptional atmospheric conditions prevailed on this ascent of Beinn Nuis, creating total cloud inversion at below 500 ft, filling the glens and blanketing the sea all around the island. Breathtaking and surreal, this rare perspective sees Mullach Mor on Holy Isle rising out of an ocean of fleecy white cloud.

The summit of Beinn Nuis affords a vista taking in Beinn Tarsuinn, Cir Mhor, The Saddle and the Goat Fell peaks, all in the finest of winter conditions.

An exquisite and rare event of nature manifests across the Kilbrannan Sound to an Atlantic horizon.
A sunkissed cotton wool quilt brushes up with the headlands and inlets of Arran's south-west corner.